Y0-DFH-780

AUSSIE SLANG
DICTIONARY

The Five Mile Press

INTRODUCTION

Our rich and colourful slang reveals a lot about the Australian national psyche. For example, it seems we don't suffer fools gladly, judging by the number of words we've coined for the dills, dingalings, drongoes, droobs and drop-kicks of this world.

Our historical ties with England are reflected in our tendency to use rhyming slang — with a distinctly Australian slant, for example, dog's eye and dead horse (pie and sauce)

Barbie, cossie, mozzie are typical examples of the national mania for abbreviating words wherever possible and adding — ie to the end. Perhaps, a sign of a benign but slightly childish streak in the national persona. Because of space restrictions, this genre has been kept to a minimum.

As well as single words, many popular phrases have been included because these give more scope for our gift for verbal inventiveness. If slang can be called folk poetry, it seems we are a highly poetic nation.

a

All alone am

act the goat
behave foolishly.

after darks
sharks (rhyming slang).

all alone like a country dunny
abandoned, lonely, alone.

all over the place like a madwoman's breakfast
in a state of chaos.

amber fluid
    beer.
ankle-biter
    toddler.
apples
    okay, all right, e.g. She'll be apples.
Aussie battler
    the ordinary Australian trying to make ends meet.
Aussie salute
    the flapping away of ever-present flies from one's face.
away with the pixies/birdies
    in another world, day-dreaming.

b

BACK o' BOURKE
A BIT FURTHER

BOURKE
A LONG WAY

back o' Bourke
> remote area of Australia.

bald as a bandicoot
> having no hair.

Banana-bender
> Queenslander.

barbie/barby
> barbecue.

Barcoo rot
> festering skin disease.

barley!
> word used to call for a truce.

barrack for
> support vocally (usually a football team).

bats
    crazy.

beaut
    extremely good, an expression of approval.

beauty!
    exclamation of approval.

beef
    complaint; to complain.

beer gut
    bulging stomach (of man) often associated with heavy beer-drinking.

bee's knees
    the best.

beg yours?
   would you mind repeating that?

bend the elbow
   to drink excessively.

berko
   crazy; furious.

bet your boots on
   to be absolutely sure about something.

better than a poke in the eye with a burnt stick
   not as bad as all that; an admission that things could be worse.

bible-basher
: clergyman, priest; religious fanatic.

big bickies
: large sum of money.

big smoke
: the city.

billies/ billy lids
: kids (rhyming slang).

bingle
: minor car accident.

bite your bum!
: shut up!; get lost!

bitser
: mongrel.

Black Stump
non-existent place in remote outback, e.g. this side of the Black Stump.

bleeder
fellow; person; bloke.

bleeding oath!
expression of unqualified agreement.

bloke
average chap, usually preceded by 'good'.

bloody
commonly known as the great Australian adjective.

bludge
    to cadge from someone else.

bludger
    one who bludges.

blue
    fight or argument; mistake.

Blue
    nickname for a redhead.

blues
    police.

bluey
    summons issued by police; cattle dog; rolled up blanket (as used by swagmen).

Bob's your uncle
expression indicating everything is fine.

bodgie
member of male subculture of the fifties, identifiable by flashy style of dress; also means inferior, unskilled.

bonzer
excellent.

boo-boo
error.

booby
timorous, foolish person.

boofhead
fool; someone with a large head.

booze artist
　heavy drinker.

booze bus
　police vehicle used to apply
　random breath-tests to drivers.

boozer
　heavy drinker; local pub.

booze-up
　wild party, with plentiful supply
　of alcohol.

bore the pants off someone
　to be excessively boring.

bosker
　excellent.

bot
>to cadge, especially cigarettes and liquor.

bottler
>person, thing or event of outstanding merit.

box of birds
>pertaining to high spirits, happiness, e.g. like a box of birds.

boys in blue
>police.

brass monkey weather
>very cold.

brass razoo
    brass farthing, i.e. small amount of money.

break it down!
    expression of disbelief.

breather
    short rest.

breeze
    easy task.

brick short of a load
    simple-minded.

bright spark
    cheerful, alert person.

brumby
    wild horse.

Buckley's
> very little chance.

buffer
> elderly man.

bugger off!
> go away!

buggerlugs
> irreverent (but sometimes affectionate) way of referring to an individual.

bugle
> nose.

built like the side of a house
> pertaining to a large, overweight person.

bull/bulldust
nonsense, rubbish.
bulldust artist
person who talks nonsense or exaggerates.
bully for you!
derisive exclamation.
bum
vulgar term for bottom.
bummer
disappointing event.
bun in the oven
pregnant.
bung
broken, damaged; to place carelessly.

burl
a try; e.g. give it a burl; to hurtle along.

bushwhacker
someone from the bush.

busy as a one-armed bill-poster in a gale
extremely busy.

butcher's (hook)
look (rhyming slang).

C

cake-hole
> mouth.

camp as a row of tents.
> of an effeminate male homosexual.

Captain Cook
> a look (rhyming slang).

cark it
> to die.

c'arn
> come on! (abbreviation), e.g. C'arn the Bombers!

carpet grub
> small child.

carry on like a pork chop
> behave in a silly way.

charge like a wounded bull
    set excessively high prices.

cheap drunk
    one who becomes intoxicated quickly.

chinwag
    a chat or gossip.

chippy
    carpenter.

chock-a-block/chockers
    full up, filled to capacity.

choof off
    to depart.

chook
    chicken, hen.

choppers
　teeth.

chuck a wobbly
　to throw a tantrum.

chunder
　vomit.

clackers
　false teeth.

climb the wall
　to go mad.

clued-up
　well-informed.

cluey
　bright, intelligent.

cobber
　mate, friend.

cockie/cocky
: cockatoo; cockroach; farmer; cheeky.

coffin-nail
: cigarette.

coldie
: can of chilled beer.

collywobbles
: feeling of apprehension.

come a cropper
: fall heavily; have a setback.

come in spinner
: call in game of two-up (Australian coin-tossing game).

comic cuts
: stomach or guts (rhyming slang).

coo-ee!
: greeting or call.

cook the books
: to illegally falsify accounts or records.

coot
: fellow (derogatory).

cossie
: swimming costume.

cot-case
: bed-ridden person.

couldn't get a kick in a stampede
: said of poorly performing football player.

couldn't knock the skin off a rice pudding
    physically weak; ineffectual.

couldn't run a chook raffle in a country pub
    incompetent.

crash-hot
    first-rate.

crawler
    sycophant.

cripes!
    exclamation.

croak
    to die.

crook
    ill; no good.

crow-eater
South Australian.

d

Dad 'n' Dave
shave (rhyming slang).

dag
  eccentric, scruffy person; a bit of a 'character'.

daggy
  someone with the attributes of a dag.

daisy-cutter
  sports term for a ball that is thrown or kicked very low.

daks
  trousers.

dead but won't lie down
  persistent where most would realise it's futile.

dead horse
  sauce (rhyming slang)

dekko
 a look.

dickhead
 foolish or obnoxious person.

digger
 returned serviceman; an Australian.

dill
 idiot.

dingaling
 silly person (affectionate).

dingbat
 foolish, eccentric person.

dinki-di
 genuine.

dipstick
: crazy, contemptible person.

dish-licker
: dog.

do a flit
: run away, especially from responsibility; move house without paying bills.

do your block
: lose your temper.

dob on (someone)
: tell tales.

doesn't know if he's/she's Arthur or Martha
: said of someone who is stupid or in a state of confusion.

dog's eye
   pie (rhyming slang)

done up like a pet lizard/done up like a pox-doctor's clerk
   dressed up; overdressed.

don't come the raw prawn
   don't pretend to be green; don't try to pull the wool over someone's eyes.

Down Under
   Australia.

drongo
   idiot.

drippy
   gormless, boring.

droob
>gormless fool.

drop a brick
>make a social blunder.

drop a clanger
>impart embarrassing information, usually unintentionally.

drop-kick
>despicable or disliked person; Australian Rules Football term.

drover's dog
>anyone at all, e.g. a drover's dog could have done it.

dry as a pom's towel
>thirsty.

duck's disease
  having short legs.

dunny
  toilet, especially outside.

e

earbasher
 someone who talks incessantly; a bore.

easy as spearing an eel with a spoon.
 very difficult.

elephants/elephant's trunk
 drunk (rhyming slang).

even-stevens
 equal chance or amount.

every bastard and his dog
 absolutely everyone.

eyes on, hands off
 admonition that it's all right to look, but not to touch.

f

face like a yard of tripe
miserable countenance.

fair crack of the whip
request for reasonable treatment.

face fungus
beard or moustache.

fair dinkum
genuine, real.

fair enough
expression used to concede a point.

fit as a trout
in excellent health.

flake out
collapse from exhaustion or intoxication.

flash as a rat with a gold tooth
    ostentatious; tastelessly over-dressed.

flicks
    films.

floater
    meat pie floating in a bowl of pea soup.

flog the cat
    to indulge in self-pity.

flophouse
    cheap boarding house; accommodation for homeless men.

flutter
    a small bet.

folding stuff
   paper money.

for crying out loud!
   expression of annoyance.

full as a fairy's phone book/full as a goog/full as a tick
   drunk; replete.

full quid
   intelligent, shrewd, quick-witted.

furphy
   unfounded rumour.

g

galah
  loudmouthed idiot.
game as Ned Kelly
  daring, brave.
gander
  a look.
g'day
  standard Australian greeting.
get on your goat
  to irritate, annoy.
get your dander up
  to become enraged.
gink
  silly person.
go crook
  lose one's temper.

go down the gurgler
  to go down the plughole, i.e. go broke, go out of business, etc.

go like the clappers
  work or move extremely fast.

go off half-cocked
  to enter an enterprise unprepared.

go walkabout
  to be missing.

goanna
  piano (rhyming slang).

gob
  mouth.

good-oh
  expression of satisfaction.

goog/googy-egg
  egg.

greaser
  flatterer, sycophant.

great Australian adjective
  the word 'bloody'.

great Australian salute
  motion of flapping ever-present flies away.

grog
  alcoholic beverages.

grotty
  dirty, unsavoury.

grouse
  excellent.

h

happy as a bastard on Father's Day
    miserable, depressed.
head like a Mini with the doors open
    to have protruding ears.
head like a robber's dog
    ugly.
heart-starter
    first alcoholic drink of the day, especially before midday.
hoon
    lout.
humdinger
    excellent, e.g. a real humdinger!
hungry as a black dog
    famished.

i

cheer up mate!

if he laughed his face would crack
   a dour individual.

iffy
>risky.

I'll be a monkey's uncle!/I'll be blowed!
>expression of surprise, amazement.

in good nick
>in good shape.

in the nick
>in jail.

I've seen a better head on a glass of beer
>insulting description of someone you consider ugly.

I wouldn't be dead for quids!
>a positive reply to 'Howya going?'

j

jam-jars
: thick-lensed spectacles.

Jesus wept!
: expression of amazement or disgust.

jiffy
: short period of time.

jiggered
: broken or of no use.

jimjams
: jitters.

Joe Blake
: snake (rhyming slang).

jumbuck
: sheep (from Aboriginal word).

k

kangaroos in the top paddock
   insane.
Kiwi
   New Zealander.
knee-high to a grasshopper
   extremely small or young.
knock your socks off
   to cause amazed admiration.
knuckle sandwich
   punch in the mouth.

1

land shark
    land speculator.

laugh at the lawn
    to vomit.

larrikin
    lout.

lie doggo
    to remain hidden (possibly to avoid work).

lights are on but there's nobody home
    said of stupid person.

like a lily on a dustbin
    lonely; neglected.

like a pick-pocket at a nudist camp
    out of place; out of one's element.
like a shag on a rock
    forlorn, lonely.
like a stunned mullet
    bewildered; inert.
like a two-bob watch
    in an erratic or crazy manner.
like billyo
    energetically, with gusto.
like the clappers
    very fast.
little beaut/little ripper
    person or thing of excellence.

loaded
:   drunk.

local-yokel
:   well-known resident.

looney bin
:   psychiatric hospital.

lousy
:   rotten; mean; wretched.

m

THOU SHALT NOT SNATCH

mackerel-snatcher
   Roman Catholic.
mad as a gumtree full of galahs
   insane.
make a proper galah of yourself
   behave foolishly.

make a quid
 earn a living.

mate
 common form of address between males; can be used affectionately or aggressively.

miffed
 annoyed, offended.

mingy
 mean, stingy.

molly the monk
 drunk (rhyming slang).

mozzie
 mosquito.

mystery bag
 sausage.

n

Ned Kelly

Ned Kelly
> belly (rhyming slang).

Never-Never
> remote Australia.

nick off
> to depart.

nicked
> stole; arrested.

ning-nong
> fool, idiot.

nipper
> small child.

no flies on (someone)
> phrase indicating person is quick-witted.

no-hoper
:   hopeless person.

no worries!
:   affirmative reply to a request for action.

Noah/Noah's ark
:   shark (rhyming slang).

nong
:   fool, simpleton.

not backward in coming forward
:   brash, pushy.

not much chop
:   not much good.

not on your nellie!
>absolutely not! under no circumstances.

not the full quid/not the full two-bob
>lacking in intelligence or sanity.

O

ocker
: uncultivated Australian man.

off like a bucket of prawns
: to depart hastily.

oldies
: parents or in-laws.

on a good thing
: to be involved in a successful venture or activity.

on a good wicket
: to have a successful (and possibly not demanding) job.

on a sticky wicket
: in trouble.

on the blink
: out of order, malfunctioning.

on the nose
:   foul-smelling.

on ya!
:   expression of encouragement.

one-armed bandit
:   poker machine.

ooroo
:   goodbye.

open slather
:   unrestricted opportunity.

outback
:   remote Australia.

outlaws
:   in-laws.

Oz
:   Australia.

p

playing possum

panic merchant
>person notorious for panicking easily.

paralytic
>extremely intoxicated.

pav/pavlova
>famous Australian dessert with meringue base.

pay through the nose
>to pay far too much.

perve
>to stare lustfully.

piece of cake
>easy task.

piker
>one who gives up easily.

pipped at the post
   narrowly beaten.

play funny-buggers/bunnies
   behave in a stupid way; to deceive or cheat.

play possum
   to feign death or sleep.

poet's day
   Friday (Piss Off Early Tomorrow's Saturday).

pom
   English person.

pong
   unpleasant smell.

poof/poofter
> offensive term for a homosexual man.

pull the other leg/one.
> expression of disbelief.

put a cork/sock in it!
> shut up!

put on a dingo act
> behave in a cowardly way.

put the mozz on (someone)
> to try to make someone make a mistake or fail.

q *quids*
large sum of money
(originally slang for pounds).

r

rare as rocking-horse shit
  extremely rare.

ratbag
  eccentric person.

rellies
  relatives (aunts, uncles, etc).

ridgie-didge
  genuine, the truth.

rough end of the pineapple
  unfair deal.

run around like a chook with its head off
  rushing about to no great effect.

S

sandgroper
  Western Australian.

sandwich short of a picnic
  lacking in intelligence.

sanger
  sandwich.

scab
  abusive term for non-union worker.

scorcher
  swelteringly hot day.

screaming heebie-jeebies
  intense irritation.

scunge
  dirty, untidy person.

scungy
: unattractive, dirty.

search me
: expression used in reply to a question you can't answer.

selling tickets on himself/herself
: expression denoting an individual is very conceited.

settler's clock
: kookaburra.

silly as a two-bob watch/silly as a wet hen/silly as a wheel
: crazy; lacking in intelligence; dizzy.

settler's clock

she'll be apples
  expression of reassurance.

sheilah
  girl; woman.

shot through like a Bondi tram
  departed hastily.

shut-eye
  sleep.

sickie
  day's sick leave (absentee is not necessarily ill).

sink a few
  to drink beer.

skedaddle
  leave hastily, flee.

skew-whiff
   askew, muddled.

skite
   boastful person; to boast.

sky pilot
   clergyman.

slacker
   lazy, irresponsible person.

smashed
   drunk.

Snake Gully
   any rustic outpost.

snag
   sausage; hidden problem.

snuff it
    to expire.

soup-strainer
    moustache.

speak on the big white telephone
    to vomit into the toilet.

spieler
    con-man, smooth talker.

spinebashing
    sleeping.

spit the dummy
    to lose your temper.

spitting chips
    enraged.

sponger
   someone who cadges from others.

spunk
   sexy, good-looking person.

squiz
   quick look.

starkers
   naked.

steak and kidney
   Sydney.

stick your bib in
   to interfere.

stickybeak
   one who pries.

still kicking
    alive (barely).
stinker
    boiling hot day.
stinko
    drunk.
stone the crows!
    exclamation.
stoney (broke)
    penniless.
stoush
    a fight; to punch, bash.
strapped for cash
    short of money.

strewth
  exclamation, usually of surprise or amazement.

strides
  trousers.

suck
  obnoxious, sycophantic person.

suss
  suspicious (abbreviation).

suss out
  to find out, surreptitiously.

sweet cop
  easy job.

sweet Fanny Adams
  zilch, none, nothing.

t

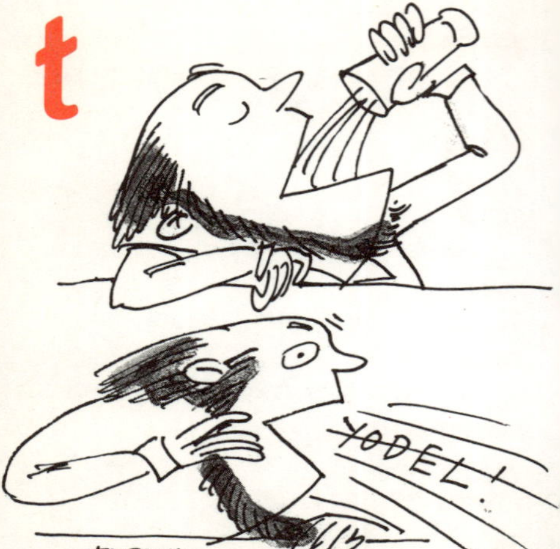

YODEL!

THROWING ONE'S VOICE
AFTER A TEN-OUNCE SANDWICH

ten-ounce sandwich
   lunch consisting of beer.

the cat's whiskers
   excellent; the best.

thick as a brick/thick as the dust on a public servant's out-tray
   stupid, dull, slow-witted.

throw (one's) voice
   to vomit.

ticker
   the heart.

tickle the till
   rob, pilfer.

tight as a fish's arse
   mean with money.

till the cows come home
    for a long time.

tinnie
    can of cold beer.

tizz
    state of confused excitement.

toey
    excitable, anxious, bad-tempered.

troppo
    crazy, insane.

true blue
    the real thing; the ultimate Aussie accolade.

turn dingo
    become an informer.

two-bob lair
: man dressed in cheap, flashy clothes.

two-pot screamer
: one who becomes quickly intoxicated.

two shakes of a lamb's/dog's tail
: in a very short time, soon.

two-up
: coin-tossing game.

underground mutton
    rabbits (when cooked).
up a gumtree
    perplexed; in trouble.
up shit creek without a paddle
    in deep trouble.
up the duff
    pregnant.
up the pole
    confused, wrong.
up there Cazaly!
    a cry of encouragement.
useful as a flywire door on a submarine
    useless.

V

verbal diarrhoea
 non-stop talk, garrulity.

W

The boat smells. It's too hot. The tea's awful. I want my £10 back.

wacker
crazy, but possibly amusing, person.
waffle
nonsense; to prattle on aimlessly.
walking papers
dismissal notice, the sack.
walloper
policeman.
welsh on
to betray, inform on; to fail to pay debts.
whacko-the-did!/whacko-the-diddle-oh!
expression of jubilation.

what do you think this is - bush week?
    rhetorical question implying the other person is acting without finesse or expertise.

whinge
    whining complaint.

whingeing pom
    dissatisfied English migrant.

whinger
    habitual complainer.

willies
    feeling of apprehension.

windy enough to blow a blue dog off its chain
    extremely windy.

wonky
> unsteady, shaky.

Woop-Woop
> fictitious remote area.

wouldn't (do something) in a pink fit
> wouldn't do something under any circumstances.

wouldn't give you the time of day
> describes uncooperative, stand-offish person.

wouldn't it rot your socks!
> exclamation of annoyance or disgust.

wouldn't know his arse from his elbow
    complete fool.

wouldn't shout in a shark attack
    of an extremely mean person.

wouldn't work in an iron lung
    of an extremely lazy person.

wowser
    person who disapproves of drinking, gambling, dancing.

yabber
to talk excessively or unintelligibly.
yahoo
uncouth lout.
yakka
physical labour.
yobbo
lout.
you're not wrong!
expression of unqualified agreement.

Z

zack
originally a sixpence, now a five cent piece.

zonked
rendered paralytic by alcohol or overwork.